MOTIVATE

A Guide to Creating
Team Member Motivation,
Enhanced Job Performance, and
Employee Satisfaction, Using the
Motivating Dynamic in Humankind

John Correll

Fulfillment Press
U.S.A.

TITLE: Motivate

SUBTITLE: A Guide to Creating Team Member Motivation, Enhanced Job Performance, and Employee Satisfaction, Using the Motivating Dynamic in Humankind

Fulfillment Press — U.S.A

Copyright © 2021 by John Correll.

Printed in the United States of America.

ISBN: 978-1-938001-74-1 - paperback
ISBN: 978-1-938001-86-4 - hardcover
Library of Congress Control Number: 2021903598
Amazon URL: amazon.com/dp/1938001869
Version: TXT: 2021-02-20 (8)   COV: 2021-02-20 (4)
Cover, text creation, formatting, editing, and proof reading by John Correll

FULFILLMENT PRESS specializes in the creation and publication of educational media for furthering personal, career, and life fulfillment. The name Fulfillment Press is a publishing imprint and registered DBA, or assumed name, of Correll Consulting, LLC.

AUTHOR: John Correll is a full-time writer. His background includes restaurant and pizzeria manager, training director, corporate VP, entrepreneur, college instructor, business consultant, and, more recently, packaging designer and inventor (holding 43 patents). The dynamics of team member motivation and performance-building have been an abiding interest of his for the past 50 years. He also enjoys fishing, hiking, and long-distance bicycling. ~ A bio of Correll is at: correllconcepts.com/correll_bio.htm

PHOTOGRAPHS: Back cover photo by Bill Bacheler.

FEEDBACK: To send gratis feedback on the book or to point out an error that possibly needs correcting, go to: correllconcepts.com/motivate2.pdf

LIMITATIONS & DISCLAIMER: Publisher, author, and distributor make no warranty or representation of any kind regarding this material and its use, and make this material available solely on an "as-is" basis. This book's purpose is to educate and entertain. It aims at a general audience. It is sold with the understanding that the author and publisher are not engaged in rendering specific personal consulting, advice, or services. The author and publisher shall have neither liability nor responsibility to any person or entity with respect to any loss or damage caused, or alleged to have been caused, directly or indirectly, by the information contained in this book.

PUBLIC SPEAKING & CONSULTING: If you're interested in exploring the possibility of retaining the author as a keynote speaker or as a consultant to your organization, go to: correllconcepts.com/consulting2.pdf

DEDICATION: To Janet Correll, one of the finest team motivators I've ever known

Contents

Preface: Why This Book Matters...5

Key Terms...6

The Core Dynamic in Team Member Motivation-building 8

Motivator #1: Make desired performance a *RAP-receiving experience*...25

Motivator #2: Make desired performance a *hassle-free pursuit*...34

Motivator #3: Make desired performance a *fun time*. 42

Motivator #4: Make desired performance a *dollar-producing endeavor*...48

Motivator #5: Make desired performance an *important accomplishment*...60

Motivator #6: Make desired performance a *winning situation*. 64

Motivator #7: Make desired performance a *personal advancement opportunity*. 67

Motivator #8: Make desired performance a *noble venture*. ...71

Motivator #9: Make desired performance a *teamship experience*...80

Motivator #10: *Reduce* the net reward connected to undesired performance...89

Core Concepts Summary...94

Preface:
Why This Book Matters

TEAM MEMBER MOTIVATION — a.k.a. employee motivation — is the biggest challenge facing organizations today. The fundamental question is: *"HOW exactly do we motivate our team members to do their job the way it needs to be done and enjoy it, too?"*

Everything a team or business does that amounts to a *lasting forward step* depends on deriving the correct answer to that question. This book discloses that answer. It identifies the core dynamic to motivation building, and then gives the top ten ways to use that dynamic to enhance team member performance and job satisfaction.

In short, team member motivation is a vital ingredient to achieving performance progress and realizing enterprise goals. That's why this book matters ... and why it was written.

Key Terms

THIS BOOK rides on two key terms: desired performance and undesired performance. Here are the definitions.

Any performance you want to occur, or to have happen, we call **desired performance.** Typically it's performance that contributes to achievement of at least one of your organization's goals or priorities. It's also sometimes called *productive performance* or *good performance.*

Any performance that's not desired performance we call **undesired performance.** Typically it's performance that does not contribute to achievement of any of your organization's goals or priorities. It's also sometimes called *poor performance* or *inadequate performance.* So, any particular performance is either desired performance or undesired performance. There's no such thing as "neutral performance."

The Terms *Team Member* and *Employee* Mean the Same

An enterprise is sustained by persons who contribute to the ongoing functioning of that enterprise. We use two terms for referring to such a person: **team member** and **employee.** We don't make a distinction between them, as we regard both to be honorable and well-meaning. In short, they're synonymous — both are referring to someone who's contributing to the ongoing functioning of an enterprise, including both managerial and non-managerial positions.

The Core Dynamic in Team Member Motivation-building

TODAY people want things distilled to simplest form. So, here is the one-sentence explanation of how to motivate team members — a.k.a. employees — to excellent job performance:

Make doing desired performance to be MORE REWARDING than doing undesired performance.

"Whoa," you say, "it's impossible for it to be that simple." But it *is* that simple. This is the core dynamic — a.k.a. the "secret" — to team member, or employee, motivation-building. Any activity, thing, condition, or program that results in getting a person to accomplish desired performance *does so* by making the execution of that desired performance to be *more rewarding* than the execution of undesired performance.

Here's why it works that way. Whenever a person confronts a choice between two mutually exclusive endeavors — such as doing desired performance versus not doing desired performance — the person almost always chooses to pursue whichever course of action appears to hold the *greater amount* of net reward for them. We call this the *Law of Performance Choice.* It's a core dynamic in humankind. So, if it happens that not doing desired performance appears to hold the greater net reward, that's the alternative that usually gets pursued!

We now come to the pivotal question facing virtually every enterprise: *How* do we get our team members to choose to pursue desired performance over undesired performance?

The answer is: We do it by *increasing the net reward of desired performance,* as team members perceive it. And how do we do that? It's in the upside versus downside of each endeavor.

Every performance holds an upside and a downside for the performer. The **upside** is whatever a performer *likes* about doing the particular performance. The **downside** is whatever the performer *dislikes* about doing it.

The *upside* can take the form of a compensation, event, communication, condition, situation, and/or opportunity the performer finds enjoyable, beneficial, or fulfilling. It can be an aspect of the performance itself <u>or</u> it can be something received afterward as a result of doing the performance.

The *downside* is anything the performer must either painfully endure or reluctantly give up in order to accomplish the performance. Things a performer might have to *endure* include difficulties, frustration, physical discomfort, psychological discomfort, fatigue, boredom, risk, and inconvenience (or hassle) involved in doing the performance. Things a performer might have to *give up* or relinquish in order to engage in the performance include personal energy, personal resources, and the opportunity to do something else instead.

Most every performance carries both an upside and a downside. So, associated with each endeavor or performance is a formula. We call it the *Net Reward Formula*, and it reads like this:

Upside – Downside = Net Reward
of the performance (for the performer)

So, the way you go about increasing the net reward of desired performance is: **(a)** expand the upside and/or **(b)** shrink the downside of doing desired performance (as viewed through the eye of the performer).

Expanded Upside and/or Shrunken Downside = GREATER NET REWARD of the Performance

You accomplish this process through two steps:

Step 1: FIND OUT what types of performance-related experiences team members like and dislike.

Step 2: INFUSE desired performance with a *greater* quantity of the experiences team members like and with a *lesser* quantity of experiences they dislike.

These two steps are the essence of team member motivation-building. We call it the *Two-step Motivation-building Process.*

So how do you do Step 1 of the Two-step Motivation-building Process, or go about finding out what types of experiences make doing desired performance more rewarding for team members? You can do it one or both of two ways: (1) You can ask them and (2) you can use trial-and-error. In the second way, you guess at what team members might like or want, then provide that thing either as *part of doing* desired performance or as a *consequence for accomplishing* desired performance (but <u>not</u> for undesired performance). Then you observe the results. If it increases the frequency, duration, or intensity with which team members pursue desired performance, you've likely found something they like. If it doesn't, it's probably not something they like.

It's easy to guess at what to try because most humans have the same basic desires. That is, most of us want to:

- Engage in enjoyable activity (and avoid uncomfortable activity).
- Feel good about our self as a person.
- Feel good about what we're doing or accomplishing.
- Feel good about our future or where we're heading.

- Earn economic reward for our efforts, especially our "extra efforts."

Or, put another way — most of us seek praise, convenience, fun, money, importance, success, advancement, nobility, and team-connection (more on these things shortly).

Once you identify the specific experiences and rewards team members enjoy and want, you then should make those things either a part of *doing* desired performance or a payoff for *accomplishing* desired performance (while taking care to avoid making those same things a part of undesired performance). All this is the essence of *Step 2* of the Two-step Motivation-building Process, which is the activity of expanding the upside and shrinking the downside of doing desired performance.

By applying the two steps of motivation-building you make doing desired performance *more rewarding* than doing undesired performance for team members. This, in turn, causes them to choose to perform a greater amount of desired performance. This is how motivation-building "happens." It's also what the upcoming Top 10 Motivators of greater team member performance are about.

But before jumping into the top ten motivators we're first going to take a brief side trip to precisely define the concepts of performance and motivation. We do this to ensure clarity and understanding.

As the term is used herein, **performance** is: human *action* and any *outcomes* that directly derive from it.

Action can take the form of either a single activity or a set of related activities. Mental and verbal processes, such as decision-making and conversation, are forms of activity. "Doing nothing" is also an activity.

An *outcome* is an object, condition, or situation resulting from human action. Here are four examples that illustrate action and outcomes.

ACTION	OUTCOME
Floor-mopping	A clean floor
Decision-making	A certain decision
Selling	A sale made
Writing	A finished report

Action + Outcomes = PERFORMANCE

In light of each company's goals there are two kinds of performance:

1. Desired Performance
2. Undesired Performance.

As we've already stated, any performance you want to occur we call **desired performance.** Typically it's performance that contributes to achievement of at least one of your organization's goals or priorities. It's also sometimes called *productive performance* or *good performance.*

Any performance that's not desired performance we call **undesired performance.** Typically it's performance that does not contribute to achievement of any of your organization's goals or priorities. It's also sometimes called *poor performance* or *inadequate performance.*

Every incident of performance is either desired performance or undesired performance. "Neutral performance" does not exist. Or, put another way, any team member at any given time is engaging in either desired performance or undesired performance. No one is ever engaging in "neutral performance" or "no performance."

As used herein, we define **motivation** as: a state of mind that causes a person to choose to engage in (or pursue) a particular task, endeavor, or performance. Further, we define **motivation-building** as: the act of creating the *conditions* that generate motivation. So relative to any particular performance you'd like to see happen, motivation-building is the act of creating the conditions that generate a state of mind that causes team members, or employees, to engage in that particular performance. Any particular condition that causes motivation we call a **motivator**.

Since you can't read minds, the only way you can know when a person has motivation for a particular desired performance is by observing their actions. If they have the wherewithal to do the performance but aren't doing it, you conclude that they're lacking the motivation necessary for doing it. On the other hand, if they're doing the performance or attempting to do it, you conclude that they *have* the motivation for it.

Finally, as previously stated, the way you create motivation within team members for accomplishing a certain desired performance is to make doing that desired performance more rewarding than doing undesired performance. This is the core dynamic — a.k.a. the "secret" — to motivation-building.

We now return to our pivotal question: *HOW do you go about making desired performance more rewarding than undesired performance?*

The way you make doing desired performance more rewarding than doing undesired performance is by applying one or more of the Top 10 Motivators of greater team member performance. We view these top ten motivators as being the ten most effective ways a leader or manager can generate an increased amount of desired performance within their enterprise or team. We start with a "short-description list," then expand it to a "one-sentence description list," and, finally, provide a full explanation of each motivator in its own separate chapter.

> **Note:** If it happens that you came to this book looking for the "top motivator" or the "top 3 motivators" or the "top 5 motivators" of excellent employee performance, you'll find them in this top 10 list. In our opinion, action #1 is the top motivator, and actions #1–3 are the top three motivators, and actions #1–5 are the top five motivators of excellent employee performance. So, if you want to do just one motivator we suggest doing #1. If you want to do only three we suggest #1–3. And if you want to do only five we suggest #1–5. Of course, for maximal results we suggest you consider applying all ten.

Top 10 Motivators in Short Form

Here, now, are the top ten motivators for creating excellent team member, or employee, performance and job satisfaction.

To make desired performance more rewarding than undesired performance, make desired performance:

1. A *RAP-receiving* experience,
2. A *hassle-free* pursuit,
3. A *fun* time,
4. A *dollar-producing* endeavor,
5. An *important* accomplishment,
6. A *winning* situation,
7. A personal *advancement* opportunity,
8. A *noble* venture, and/or
9. A *teamship* experience.

    Plus ...

10. *Reduce* the net reward of <u>un</u>desired performance.

Motivators #1–9 involve expanding the net reward of desired performance. Motivator #10 involves reducing the net reward of undesired performance.

It's also possible to distill motivators #1–9 to one word each. It reads like this.

To make desired performance more rewarding than undesired performance, infuse desired performance with:

1. Praise,
2. Convenience,
3. Fun,
4. Money,
5. Importance,
6. Success,
7. Advancement,
8. Nobility, and/or
9. Teamship.

Top 10 Motivators in One-sentence Description

Now we expand each of the above short descriptions into a sentence.

To make desired performance more rewarding than undesired performance, apply (one or more of) the following ten motivators:

**MOTIVATOR 1: Make desired performance a *RAP-receiving experience* for team members by delivering sincere Recognition, Appreciation, or Praise whenever someone either accomplishes desired performance *or* engages in "right actions" — a.k.a. performance progress (p. 25).

MOTIVATOR 2: Make desired performance a *hassle-free pursuit* for team members by identifying and eliminating the needless aggravations and inconveniences associated with doing desired performance (p. 34).

MOTIVATOR 3: Make desired performance a *fun time* for team members by, as much as possible, matching each one to a job and tasks that involve activities the person innately enjoys doing (p. 42).

MOTIVATOR 4: Make desired performance a *dollar-producing endeavor* for team members by installing a differential pay program or, in other words, by paying a person more when they accomplish a greater amount of desired performance than when they accomplish the "usual amount" or "standard amount" (p. 48).

MOTIVATOR 5: Make desired performance an *important accomplishment* for team members by paying personal attention to the performing of desired performance by them (p. 60).

MOTIVATOR 6: Make desired performance a *winning situation* for team members by structuring desired performance into a series of desired goals, then arranging for them to succeed in accomplishing these goals, and, finally, celebrate after each instance of goal achievement (p. 64).

MOTIVATOR 7: Make desired performance a *personal advancement opportunity* for team members by creating an intra-position advancement system that makes an automatic connection between sustained desired performance by a person and the person's personal advancement (p. 67).

MOTIVATOR 8: Make desired performance a *noble venture* for team members by you personally committing to making your business enterprise or organizational unit the best at what it does (p. 71).

MOTIVATOR 9: Make desired performance a *teamship experience* for team members by arranging for them to have the opportunity to contribute to overall team performance and success, and then to receive appreciation from team members for doing that (p. 80).

MOTIVATOR 10: Reduce the net reward of <u>un</u>desired performance by identifying any upside for team members that might be associated with doing undesired performance, and then reducing or eliminating that upside (p. 89).

TOP 10 MOTIVATORS – The Whole Picture

We now come to the full explanation of how to use the top ten motivators to make desired performance more rewarding than undesired performance and, thereby, motivate team members — a.k.a. employees — to more frequently choose to pursue desired performance over undesired performance. We describe each motivator in a separate chapter.

Remember this for the rest of your life. The core dynamic in motivating team members to excellent job performance is: **Make doing desired performance to be MORE REWARDING than doing undesired performance.**

When doing desired performance is more rewarding than doing undesired performance, desired performance HAPPENS.

Motivator **#1** is a way to bring this about.

Motivator #1:
Make desired performance a
RAP-receiving experience.

THIS MOTIVATION-BUILDER is likely the most important of all. If a manager does this and nothing more, the incidence of desired performance in their team will *increase!*

RAP stands for **R**ecognition, **A**ppreciation, and **P**raise. Although similar, there's a slight distinction between these three things:

Recognition = *Awareness* and approval of something we've done.

Appreciation = *Thanks* for doing it.

Praise = *Commendation* for doing it exceptionally well.

Receiving any one of the three is gratifying to most of us. However, it's possible to combine all three for maximum effect. Here's an example:

"I noticed what you just did [recognition].
That's exceptional work [praise].
Thanks a lot [appreciation]."

Humans enjoy receiving RAP. For many of us it's our biggest motivator at work or, at the least, second only to cash.

Unfortunately, as powerful as RAP is, most leaders and managers use it sparingly. The reason they state for doing so is: "Team members already get too much praise ... and if I praise them before they achieve the goal (or complete the entire task), they'll become de-motivated and stop working toward the goal."

This reasoning might sound logical. But it's incorrect. To prove it to yourself, go up to *any* group of workers — salaried or hourly, leadership or non-leadership — and say the following: "Would everyone here who has been receiving too much praise from their boss please raise your hand." You know what — almost no one raises their hand. Because no one believes they're receiving too much *sincere* recognition, appreciation, and praise. Contrary to what many leaders and managers surmise, RAP is not overused. Instead, it's one of the most *underused* motivators in the workplace today. Virtually everyone loves RAP; virtually no one receives close to as much as they would like. In short, no one gets so much of it they're "tired of it."

So, you should seek out instances of RAP-deserving performance by team members and, whenever you find it, promptly deliver <u>sincere</u> recognition, appreciation, and/or praise.

WHEN You Should Deliver RAP

For maximum effect, don't wait until the "big goal" is achieved before giving RAP. Instead, dispense RAP "along the way." In other words, make performance *progress* a RAP-receiving experience for team members. **Performance progress** is any occasion when a team member's performance moves closer to a particular performance standard or goal. Accordingly, "right actions" are a form of performance progress. The following things are right actions:

- A successful first step in a new endeavor;
- Doing a particular thing "right" for a first time;
- Giving unusual diligence in pursuit of desired performance;

- Doing something extra that furthers team progress;

- Moving to a higher level of proficiency in some aspect of desired performance;

- Continuing to extend a series or "streak" of good performance for another day or week.

The main idea is: You should focus on "rapping" right actions because the more RAP team members receive for right actions the more they enjoy doing right actions. And, the more they enjoy doing right actions the more right actions they do. And, the more right actions they do the quicker and more effectively the team or enterprise achieves its overall goals.

This happens because (a) performance progress is the pathway to goal achievement and (b) RAP is a primary motivator of performance progress. In other words ...

RAP → More Performance Progress → Quicker Goal Achievement

It's that simple.

HOW You Should Deliver RAP

RAP can vary in its degree of impact — some instances being highly motivating, others less so. What determines its degree of impact is *how* it's delivered. Behavioral psychology has created a list of rules for maximizing the motivating impact of positive reinforcement (which is what RAP is). By delivering RAP according to these rules you increase its effect on motivating team members to deliver right actions and desired performance.

Delivering RAP for Maximum Effect

For your RAP to have maximum effect, make it like this:

- **Sincere.** Mean what you say and say only what you mean. If you don't believe it, don't say it. People tend to sense when someone is lying to them. So sincerity, or truthfulness, is Rule #1 for delivering effective RAP. It's because lying is a form of disrespect and disrespect is a de-motivator. Which means, insincere RAP is worse than no RAP at all.

  > **Note:** Whenever the rare instance occurs where someone says they're receiving too much positive

reinforcement, what they're probably referring to is too many *insincere* compliments — a.k.a. flattery and BS.

- **Specific.** Tell the person *exactly* what they did that you liked. In other words, state the *specific* actions or outcomes that earned them the RAP. "Generalized RAP" can sound like BS, and that's not good.

- **Immediate.** Deliver RAP as soon as possible after spotting the right action. The longer the delay, the smaller the impact will be on motivating repeat performance.

- **Frequent.** Don't be stingy with it. *Every* step forward — every act of personal progress or performance improvement — deserves some RAP.

- **Personalized and Individualized.** Use your own words and style — express how *you* feel as opposed to how the company or "management" feels. And when delivering RAP to a group, try to give it to individuals, as well.

  Note: Some persons dislike receiving public recognition, or having the spotlight put on them in a group setting. So, for these persons you should

> dispense their recognition privately rather than publicly.

- **Varied and Random.** Avoid saying the same thing every time you give praise. Also, avoid praising the same team member for the same thing at the same time every day. "Routinized RAP" smacks of insincerity. And, as we've said, insincere-sounding RAP is worse than no RAP at all. So make your RAP creative and spontaneous.

- **Separate from Criticism.** Don't combine criticism with RAP. Doing so reduces the enjoyment and motivating effect of the RAP for the team member. Give any criticism and "bad news" at another time.

- **Occasionally Combine with a Tangible Reward.** For extra impact in special situations, give a "token of your appreciation" along with the RAP. Use this for spotlighting right actions that are extra-important and that you very much want a team member to repeat. The reward need not be expensive — a movie ticket, $5 gift certificate, or even just a $1.00 coin are examples.

Note: The purpose of the reward is to *express your appreciation*, not to replace it. So keep the focus on your appreciation as opposed to the object.

To Sum Up ...

Be on the lookout for right actions by team members. And each time you see one, provide Recognition, Appreciation, or Praise. By doing this you increase the enjoyment (or net reward) team members derive from doing right actions. Which, in turn, builds their motivation to continue doing them.

In our opinion, this Motivator #1 is the most effective motivator in creating a high-performance enterprise. Applying it will greatly increase the amount of desired performance in most teams. However, if you'd like to generate still further motivation in team members consider also applying one or more of the following Motivators #2–10.

Always remember — the "secret" to motivating team members to excellent job performance is:

Make doing desired performance to be MORE REWARDING than doing undesired performance.

When doing desired performance is more rewarding than doing undesired performance, desired performance HAPPENS.

Motivator **#2** is a way to bring this about.

Motivator #2:
Make desired performance a *hassle-free pursuit.*

AS PREVIOUSLY EXPLAINED, every endeavor has an upside, a downside, and a measure of net reward as expressed by the formula:

Upside – Downside = Amount of Net Reward

So one way you can increase the net reward of a particular performance is by shrinking the downside — that is, reducing the difficulties, frustration, discomfort, fatigue, boredom, risk, inconvenience, and lost resources — that's incurred by the performer in doing the performance.

For most performances the downside comes in two parts: *Necessary* and *Needless.*

Necessary downside is the part that's vital to accomplishing the performance. In other words, without it the performance couldn't be completed, or at least not completed well.

Needless downside, on the other hand, is the part that's non-vital to the performance. In other words, if it were eliminated the performance could still be accomplished. We call this aspect of downside "hassle." **Hassle** connected to desired performance reduces the enjoyment (or net reward) of the performance for the performer. Which, in turn, reduces the person's motivation to accomplish the performance.

*So, you should identify and eliminate needless hassle that's associated with doing desired performance! Or, put another way, you should make doing desired performance as **easy and convenient as possible.***

By doing this you decrease the downside and, thereby, increase the net reward of desired performance. Which, in turn, builds team members' motivation for doing the performance.

Needless hassle comes in four main forms: (1) needless hassle-creating policies and procedures, (2) lack of understanding of what desired performance comprises, (3) lack of personal ability to do desired performance, and (4) lack of resources needed for doing desired performance easily. We'll describe each.

How to Eliminate Needless Hassle-creating Procedures

Needless hassle-creating policies and procedures can be an "invisible" but powerful downside to doing desired performance. So you should strive to eliminate them. There are three main ways of identifying needless hassle-creating policies and procedures: (1) *experience* the job yourself (for a day or two), or (2) *observe* it being done, or (3) *ask* team members "How could your job be made easier and less hassle-filled?"

Even with that, spotting hassle can be tricky. This is because it often appears under the headings of "company policy" and "standard operating procedure." When first installed, a procedure might be necessary but, over time, becomes needless without anyone recognizing it. So, identifying hassle requires constant scrutiny of those things that are assumed to be "given" and "necessary."

Once identified, eliminate the needless policies and procedures associated with doing desired performance. Doing this might require persistence. This is because it often entails someone having to make a change in procedure or thinking — a formidable hurdle in any situation.

How to Eliminate Lack of Awareness, Lack of Ability, and Lack of Resources

In addition to outdated, nonproductive policies and procedures, three other factors also cause job aggravation and hassle for a team member: (1) *lack of awareness* by the team member of what exactly constitutes desired performance, (2) *lack of personal ability* to accomplish desired performance with ease and proficiency, and (3) *lack of adequate tools and resources* for doing the job easily and correctly.

The three fixes for these three frustrating conditions involve three actions: (1) *describing* desired performance — that is, precisely describing what desired performance comprises or "looks like," (2) *training* for desired performance — that is, training team members in the personal skills needed to do their job well (typically on-the-job training), and (3) *equipping* for desired performance — that is, providing team members with all the tools and resources needed for achieving performance excellence. Action #1 creates *awareness* of what desired performance consists of. Action #2 creates the personal *ability* to do desired performance. Action #3 provides the *resources* necessary for doing desired performance easily and expeditiously. We'll describe how to do each.

Action #1 – DESCRIBING: To convey an effective description of desired performance, describe desired performance in terms of the *whole* picture. The "whole picture" consists of two parts:

1. The MACRO view — this includes the *overall* objective of the performance (or job) plus any strategy considerations.

2. The MICRO view — this includes the *specific* actions and outcomes needed for achieving the overall objective.

The macro view communicates the broad perspective. The micro view communicates the details. For a team member to grasp the whole performance picture, *both* views must be imparted.

Action #2 – TRAINING: To train team members with the skills to achieve desired performance, conduct on-the-job training by way of these five steps — Describe, Demonstrate, Review, Reinforce, Repeat. Here's how.

1. DESCRIBE the performance to be learned.

2. DEMONSTRATE how to do it — that is, you or a skilled team member do it.

3. Have the trainee try the performance. Then REVIEW — or explain — (a) what they did well and, if needed, (b) what area or aspect they need to gain further skill in.

4. REINFORCE the trainee for what they did correctly or well. (See "How You Should Deliver RAP," page 29, for how to easily do this.)

5. If needed, REPEAT steps 2–4 until the trainee can readily perform the desired performance.

Action #3 – EQUIPPING: To equip team members with the resources required for doing desired performance, first do one or more of these three actions:

1. EXPERIENCE the performance yourself,

2. OBSERVE it being done,

3. ASK team members "What could you use that would enable you to do your job more easily and effectively?"

Then provide team members with what they need.

To Sum Up ...

Be diligent in eliminating hassle associated with doing desired performance. You do this by (a) eliminating needless hassle-creating policies and procedures involved in doing desired performance, (b) describing the whole performance picture, (c) conducting on-the-job training, and (d) equipping team members with all the tools and resources necessary for easily accomplishing desired performance.

By doing this you shrink the downside of doing desired performance and, thereby, increase the enjoyment (or net reward) team members derive from doing it. Which, in turn, helps build their motivation to accomplish desired performance.

Don't forget — the "secret" to motivating team members to excellent job performance is:
Make doing desired performance to be MORE REWARDING than doing undesired performance.

When doing desired performance is more rewarding than doing undesired performance, desired performance HAPPENS.

Motivator **#3** is a way to bring this about.

Motivator #3:
Make desired performance a
fun time.

EVERY JOB or task consists of a particular set of activities. In the eye of each performer each of these activities is either *enjoyable* or *non-enjoyable*. So for each team member, each job consists of X percent of enjoyable activities and 100–X percent of non-enjoyable activities. The greater the percent of enjoyable activities in a particular job, the greater the pleasure (or net reward) the team member derives from doing the job.

However, humans differ in their affinity for performing various types of activities. What one person loves another hates. Which means, the percent of enjoyable activity contained in any particular type of job differs from team member to team member.

So, to maximize the net reward team members derive from doing their job, you should — as much as possible — match them to jobs and tasks that involve activities they **innately enjoy doing.**

By doing this you increase the enjoyment (or net reward) team members derive from performing their job. Which, in turn, helps maintain their motivation to stick with their job and perform it well.

How to Find Out What Team members Enjoy Doing

So, when there's a choice of two or more jobs to be done, *ask* the team member which one they would prefer to take on. This is the easiest way to find out what a person enjoys doing.

Another way of finding out what team members like is by *observing* them in action. When a person is pursuing an activity with tireless effort and a smile it usually means they enjoy the activity. When they're having trouble mustering energy and a smile, it usually means they find the activity to be non-enjoyable.

Lastly, there's the situation where a job or task contains activities a person not only doesn't enjoy, but actually dislikes. This can be troublesome because us humans tend to "screw up" and "forget to do" those activities we find to be objectionable. In a situation where there's only one type of job and it contains some activities that are objectionable to most persons, you might try one or both of these two strategies.

First, try eliminating the disliked activities by changing a procedure or by "designing or automating the objectionable activity out of existence."

Second, try expanding the job to include additional activities the team member likes doing. If possible, arrange for the "disliked activities" to come first, followed by the "liked activities." This way the enjoyable activities serve as positive reinforcement for completing the unpleasant ones.

Team Member Recruitment

An additional way to increase the level of work enjoyment within your team is to apply *selective recruitment*. In other words, during the process of selecting a person for filling a particular job position, hire only those who would *enjoy* (or at least not dislike) performing the main activities involved in that position. A recruitment or consulting firm might be helpful in constructing a "test" for assisting you in determining the degree to which any particular job applicant is predisposed to liking the activities involved in a particular job.

Another way of matching a person to a job is to describe for the person the *specific activities* involved in the job, and then observe the person's response. Also, you might follow up with this question: *"On a scale of 1 to 5, with 1 being 'no enjoyment' and 5 being 'high enjoyment,' in your opinion <u>how much</u> would you enjoy doing the activities I just described?"* A person who answers "4" or "5" is probably more apt to enjoy that particular job than one who answers "1" or "2" (assuming they're giving honest answers).

To Sum Up ...

As much as feasible, match team members to jobs involving activities they innately enjoy doing. By doing this you increase the enjoyment (or net reward) that most team members derive from doing desired performance. Which, in turn, makes it easier for them to "eagerly jump into" their job and excel at it.

In our opinion, Motivators #1–3 constitute the "Top Three Motivators" in performance-building:

1 – Make desired performance a *RAP-receiving experience;*

2 – Make desired performance a *hassle-free pursuit;*

3 – Make desired performance a *fun time.*

These three motivators form the foundation of a high-performance enterprise. When combined with Motivators #4 and #5, super things can happen.

Keep in mind — the "secret" to motivating team members to excellent job performance is:

Make doing desired performance to be MORE REWARDING than doing undesired performance.

When doing desired performance is more rewarding than doing undesired performance, desired performance HAPPENS.

Motivator **#4** is a way to bring this about.

Motivator #4:
Make desired performance a
dollar-producing endeavor.

WHEN A PERSON receives something they like as a result of something they've done, they will likely *repeat* whatever they did that resulted in getting that something they like.

This cause-effect dynamic is validated by over a half-century of behavioral research. It's now considered to be a *fact*. And common sense confirms it, too. We all know that when we receive something we like as a result of something we've done, we tend to repeat what we did in anticipation of getting more of what we like.

What this means is: If you want to motivate a person or group to continue a particular performance, one way of accomplishing this is to give them something they like as a *consequence* of doing the performance.

This process of giving someone something they like as a consequence for a performance is known as *reinforcement,* often called positive reinforcement. And that "something they like" is known as a *reinforcer,* sometimes called a reward.

> **Note:** Do not confuse providing a reinforcer with providing an incentive. An incentive is a *promise* to deliver a particular thing if the performer delivers a particular performance. It's provided *before* the performance occurs. A reinforcer, on the other hand, is a *reward* that's received for actually accomplishing the performance. It's provided *after* the performance occurs. The logic behind an incentive is: "If you do X, I'll give you Y." The logic behind a reinforcer is: "Because you did X, you're getting Y."

In the work setting there are four categories of reinforcers:

1. **Tangibles,** which are physical and economic things the performer can use.

2. **Communication,** which mainly is verbal communication between others and the performer.

3. **Activities,** which are actions and events the performer can do or engage in.

4. Opportunities, which are situations and conditions that could result in the performer obtaining something they desire.

So, a reinforcer is an enjoyment-producing thing, communication, activity, or opportunity given as a *consequence* for a particular performance. Reinforcers are widely used in motivation-building. For example, five of these top ten motivators make use of reinforcers. Motivator #1 uses RAP, which is a verbal communication reinforcer. Motivator #6 uses winning moments, which is an activity reinforcer. Motivator #7 uses personal advancement opportunity, which is an opportunity reinforcer. This Motivator #4 uses one of the most powerful reinforcers of all: money — a tangibles reinforcer. And, Motivator #9 uses teamship experience, which is an activity reinforcer.

Greater Contingency → Greater Motivation

In every enterprise, every form of employee compensation is either contingent or non-contingent on accomplishment of desired performance.

Contingent compensation is compensation that's acquired by a person only when the person performs a certain desired performance. So, when the person performs the certain desired performance they get the certain compensation. And, when they don't perform the certain desired performance they <u>don't</u> get the compensation.

Non-contingent compensation, on the other hand, is compensation that's acquired by a person regardless of whether or not they accomplish a certain desired performance. So, when the person performs the certain desired performance they get the certain compensation. <u>And</u>, when they *don't* perform the certain performance they *still* get the compensation.

A way to build team members' motivation for doing a certain desired performance is to have a compensation system by which a person automatically gets a greater amount of compensation when they do the desired performance than when they don't do it.

Or, put another way, to increase team members' motivation for accomplishing a certain desired performance, increase the amount (or percent) of compensation that's contingent on doing the desired performance (and, conversely, decrease the amount that's non-contingent on doing the performance).

This explains why, in most organizations, pay is not a motivator of desired performance. It's because, in most companies all pay is *non-contingent* on desired performance. Or, put another way, in most companies employees receive as much compensation for lesser-desired performance as they receive for greater-desired performance.

In order for pay to be a motivator of a greater amount of desired performance, doing a greater amount of desired performance must result in *greater pay* than doing the "usual amount" of desired performance.

*So, you should consider paying a team member **more** when they accomplish a greater* *amount of desired performance than when they accomplish the "usual amount."*

Doing this results in a portion of employee pay being contingent on doing desired performance. This increases the net reward of desired performance for employees. Which, in turn, builds their motivation to accomplish (a greater amount of) desired performance.

A compensation system in which (a portion of) compensation is contingent on performing desired performance we call a *differential pay program.*

There are many ways a differential pay program can be applied. No one way is best for all companies or situations because a differential pay program must accommodate the unique goals and functions of each particular enterprise. So, creating an optimal program is a refinement process done by trial-and-error.

Regardless, applying the following guidelines will likely increase the motivational effect of most differential pay programs.

Guidelines for an Effective Differential Pay Program

1. CREATE a pay system consisting of two parts: (1) a *base pay* given for "base performance" and (2) a *performance bonus* given for "bonus performance." The two should add up to a total compensation amount that's competitive within your industry or market.

2. MAKE the performance bonus at least 15 percent of the total pay. For example, if base pay is, say, $10.00 per hour, the performance bonus might be an additional $1.50 per hour (or more).

3. MAKE the performance period the same as the pay period, typically either one week or two weeks. If you have a longer pay period, consider having several performance periods within the pay period, with each performance period having its own bonus opportunity.

4. ISSUE the performance bonus *with each paycheck*.

5. BASE the bonus on a simple, unambiguous performance criterion or set of criteria.

"Unambiguous" means open to one possible interpretation only. Here are samples of simple, unambiguous performance criterions. Any one or a combination of which could serve as criteria for a performance bonus:

- Number of days worked as scheduled (i.e., without tardiness or absence)

- Number of days worked wearing the complete correct uniform

- Average customer satisfaction score derived from customer feedback surveys

- "Average team contribution score" derived from team member feedback surveys in which each team member numerically rates each of the other team members on their overall contribution to the team's productivity

- Personal development as measured by a test score of some new skill or knowledge area

- Average number of units produced or delivered per hour or per day

- Average number of customers served per hour or per day
- Average transaction amount
- Average product quality score based on an objective quality measurement method
- And so on.

6. BE SURE to base the bonus on performance that's *controllable by team members*. Avoid pinning the bonus to something they only partially control the outcome of. Which means, if any of the above examples of performance criterion aren't controllable by your employees, don't use that criterion.

7. MAKE SURE team members know *how much bonus they earned* in each pay period. Pay the bonus with a separate "bonus check" *or* show the bonus amount on a separate "bonus" line on the stub of the regular pay-check.

8. MAKE SURE team members know *what specific performance* the bonus is for. Getting a bonus without knowing why has no motivating value.

9. NEVER issue the bonus to an employee who didn't earn it. In other words, never pay a bonus to a person who failed to meet the pre-established bonus performance criterion.

Comments

Many things can sabotage a differential pay program. To create an effective program requires trial-and-error. After each test period, keep what's working and replace what isn't with something new. Then test again. Eventually perfection arrives.

Many variations are possible. For example, you can base the performance bonus either on individual performance or on team performance, or on *both*. Basing it on team performance can provide the benefit of creating peer encouragement to under-performers (a.k.a. bonus detractors) to bring their substandard performance up to par.

You also can use a revolving bonus criteria, where (a portion of) the criteria changes every month or so. This injects variety and newness into team members' jobs. It also helps broaden their focus and abilities.

Lastly, you can apply a sliding scale to the bonus criteria. For example, employees could get full bonus for meeting the full bonus criteria, half bonus for coming just slightly short of the full criteria, and no bonus for falling substantially short of the criteria. What constitutes "slightly short" and "substantially short" should be defined by specific criteria, or "hard numbers." An advantage of a sliding scale is that it keeps a person from giving up after one stumble or the first bad day.

For more info on the principles of behavioral psychology and how to use positive reinforcement in the workplace, check out the book *Performance Management* by Aubrey Daniels.

To Sum Up ...

Consider putting your money where your mouth is. Consider installing a differential pay program — a program that enables each employee to get a larger paycheck when they accomplish a "bonus" performance criteria during the pay period. By doing this you increase the payoff (or net reward) that team members derive from accomplishing desired performance. Which, in turn, builds their motivation for continuing to accomplish it.

Never forget — the "secret" to motivating team members to excellent job performance is:

Make doing desired performance to be MORE REWARDING than doing undesired performance.

When doing desired performance is more rewarding than doing undesired performance, desired performance HAPPENS.

Motivator **#5** is a way to bring this about.

Motivator #5:
Make desired performance an
important accomplishment.

VIRTUALLY EVERYONE likes feeling important!
So what enables a team member to feel that way?
The equation is simple: A person who does
important things is important; a person who
does unimportant things is *un*important. In
other words:

> *Doing important things =*
> *Being an important person.*

So for a team member to feel important they
must feel like they're doing *important things*.

This leads to the crucial question: In a team
situation, what makes a particular activity
important? The answer: An activity is important
when it's considered to be important by the
team's leadership.

So how does a team member know which
activities the team leadership regards as
important? A person knows which activities are
important by observing what the leadership *pays*

attention to. In other words, from the perspective of most team members:

Leadership Attention =
Performance Importance

So, you should pay **personal attention** *to the performing of desired performance by your team members.*

And how do you do that? You take time to get *personally* involved with it. In other words, you frequently take time to *explain, train, observe,* and/or *respond* to desired performance. That's all there is to it. What the leader pays personal attention to is seen as important by team members. What the leader doesn't pay attention to is viewed as unimportant.

To Sum Up ...

Consider creating instances in which you pay *personal attention* to desired performance by team members. For example, you might consider spending at least a few minutes each day *personally observing and responding to* some particular desired performance of one or more team members (rotating between team members from day to day). Because, when you pay personal attention to someone's desired performance you raise the *importance* of that performance in the eyes of that person. And by doing this you increase the enjoyment (or net reward) the person derives from doing the performance. Which, in turn, builds their motivation to continue doing it. Very simple!

In our opinion, Motivators #1–5 constitute the "Top Five Motivators" in a high-performance enterprise:

1 – Make desired performance a *RAP-receiving experience;*

2 – Make desired performance a *hassle-free pursuit;*

3 – Make desired performance a *fun time;*

4 – Make desired performance a *dollar-producing endeavor;*

5 – Make desired performance an *important accomplishment.*

Know this — the "secret" to motivating team members to excellent job performance is:

Make doing desired performance to be MORE REWARDING than doing undesired performance.

When doing desired performance is more rewarding than doing undesired performance, desired performance HAPPENS.

Motivator **#6** is a way to bring this about.

Motivator #6:
Make desired performance a
winning situation.

A **WINNING SITUATION** is a situation that's filled with winning moments. A *winning moment* is a point in time when a person succeeds at reaching a desired goal and enjoys it.

Humans like winning moments. So winning moments can be used to enhance the net reward of a particular performance for a performer and, as a result, build the performer's motivation to accomplish the performance.

So, you should consider structuring desired performance into a series of desired goals, then arrange for team members to <u>succeed in achieving those goals</u>, and finally <u>celebrate</u> after the achievement of each goal. Or, in short, you should infuse desired performance with winning moments.

In a nutshell, here's how to do it.

1. **CREATE** a challenging-but-attainable performance goal, a graph for charting progress toward the goal, and a team action plan having numerous sub-goals, or milestones, leading to the main goal.

2. **EQUIP** team members with the awareness, ability, and resources to achieve the sub-goals. (See "How to Eliminate Lack of Awareness ...", pgs. 37–40, for details on how to do this.)

3. **CHART** performance progress and provide words of praise — or RAP — for progress and right actions. (See Motivator #1 for greater detail.)

4. **CELEBRATE** upon reaching each sub-goal. Each time you do this it's a *winning moment*. A series of periodic winning moments makes performance progress fun and rewarding.

Through these four steps you can turn team members' work into a *fun game*.

To Sum Up ...

Consider structuring team members' work situation — or the pursuit of desired performance —

into a series of winning moments. By doing this you increase the enjoyment — or net reward — team members derive from pursuing desired performance. Which, in turn, builds their motivation for continuing to achieve it.

Always remember — the "secret" to motivating team members to excellent job performance is:
Make doing desired performance to be MORE REWARDING than doing undesired performance.

When doing desired performance is more rewarding than doing undesired performance, desired performance HAPPENS.

Motivator **#7** is a way to bring this about.

Motivator #7:
Make desired performance a _personal advancement opportunity._

MOST OF US enjoy the feeling that accompanies personal progress and development. And personal advancement in our job is one of the ways we can realize that personal progress. Indeed, many of us would give above-average effort to gain that feeling if the opportunity was there. However, in most companies the opportunities for personal advancement are few and far between.

So, you should consider creating an intra-position advancement system that makes an **automatic connection** between sustained good performance by a team member and that team member's personal advancement <u>within</u> their job position.

For this to work, everyone must recognize the following cause-effect dynamic:

How to Create This Connection

Traditionally, people view advancement as *inter*position advancement — that is, moving from one job position to another. Such moves occur <u>in</u>frequently for the majority of employees. This is because there are a limited number of position-to-position advancement opportunities available in most companies (especially if your boss happens to be close to the same age as you and is perfectly suited for and content within their present position).

So how do you overcome this problem? Answer: You install *intra-position* advancement — that is, upward movement *within* a particular job position. To do this do these three things. First, define multiple levels of professional accomplishment within each job position. Second, attach to each level a particular title, pay grade, and/or set of perks. Third, define a performance criteria that's required for achieving each level.

Through such a program you enable team members to achieve advancement *within* their job position by providing sustained good performance (i.e., sustained desired performance) over the period of their employment in that position.

The advancement criteria for this intra-position advancement program should be challenging-but-attainable. In other words, it should be tough enough that a person cannot qualify by way of substandard performance but not so tough that the criteria can't be satisfied with a reasonable amount of effort or sustained desired performance.

In short, you should make it possible for a worthy, good-performing employee to be able to qualify for intra-position advancement at least once or twice each year, with the first advancement or two perhaps coming a little sooner, for the purpose of "jumpstarting the advancement-reward process."

To Sum Up ...

Consider setting up an Intra-position Advancement System that rewards consistently good-performing team members with periodic intra-position advancement. By doing this you increase the payoff (or net reward) they derive from their sustained good performance. Which, in turn, builds their motivation to deliver more of it.

Always bear in mind — the "secret" to motivating team members to excellent job performance is:

Make doing desired performance to be MORE REWARDING than doing undesired performance.

When doing desired performance is more rewarding than doing undesired performance, desired performance HAPPENS.

Motivator #8 is a way to bring this about.

Motivator #8:
Make desired performance a
noble venture.

SOMETHING IS *NOBLE* when it possesses high character or extraordinary merit. Most persons derive satisfaction from being involved in a noble venture — so much so they will support what they regard to be a noble venture with conviction and, at times, considerable sacrifice.

*So, if you were to turn your enterprise into a NOBLE VENTURE it would give many team members an opportunity to derive a deeper measure of personal satisfaction from their desired performance, because their desired performance would be viewed as something contributing to the success of the noble venture. This would enable team members to view their desired performance as an **act of nobleness.***

How to Turn Your Team Activity, or Business Enterprise, into a Noble Venture

The process of creating a noble venture is simple. But implementing it requires sincerity, commitment, and sacrifice on the part of team leadership. This is because, when it comes to nobility it's all or nothing. Either an endeavor is noble or it isn't. There's no such thing as "partial nobility" or "sometime nobility" or "pseudo-nobility." So if you intend to adopt this particular motivator, you first have some soul-searching to do and a personal commitment to make. Otherwise, it will fail.

To turn your enterprise into a noble venture, apply these seven steps.

1. Make it your personal mission to be the leader (manager, owner) of *the best* team, store, department, or business in your market, region, industry, or company. This likely will require extra work and sacrifice. If for whatever reason you can't or don't want to make this personal commitment and sacrifice, stop here and proceed to the next motivator.

Note: We're talking about being the best, not the biggest. Nobility is a quality, not a quantity. Of course there's nothing wrong with being the biggest. It's just not the topic here.

2. Translate your personal mission into a concise sentence or statement that will become your team's point of pride and rallying cry. You can call it your Team Mission, if you like. Or you could call it your *Point of Pride*. This statement now becomes the reason or justification for why every team member should perform their job to a particular level of performance excellence.

3. Write out a *Performance Excellence Job Description* for each job position on the team. Describe the type (or level) of desired performance that's required in each position for achieving the team's Point of Pride. Each description should contain two parts: (1) the *Overriding Objective* of the position and (2) a description of the *Specific Action and Outcomes* necessary for achieving the Objective.

4. Convey the Performance Excellence Job Descriptions to your team. In addition, provide whatever training and resources they need for doing the performance described in the Job Descriptions. (See "How to Eliminate Lack of Awareness ...", pgs. 37–40, for details on how to do this.)

5. Communicate the Point of Pride to your team on an *ongoing* basis. Communicate it orally and in writing. Include it as part of every communication, as much as feasible. Let your team members know on a *frequent* basis that it's your *fervent* desire and personal mission for your team to be THE BEST at what it does — or to realize the team's Point of Pride to the furthest extent possible.

6. Personally demonstrate exemplary performance on a *daily* basis. In other words, personally embody the type of attitude, commitment, and desired performance that every team member must provide in order for your team (store, department, business) to achieve its Point of Pride. Similarly, base every decision and communication you make on the Point of Pride. The foundation of a noble venture is *leadership integrity* (that is, leading by example — walking the talk and talking the walk). Hypocrisy is anti-productive, so it's not allowed here. This step, along with upcoming Step 7, is the crux of the process.

7. Don't condone or overlook deliberate recurring undesired performance by any team member. Such performance we call *anti-noble performance*. Of course, everyone has an occasional accident, oversight, or unintentional mishap. And most everyone occasionally lapses into a moment of inadequate or less-than-great performance. But that's different from *deliberate recurring* undesired performance. Basically, if a person knows *what* they should be doing and has the *resources* and *skills* to do it but is routinely not doing it, then they are engaging in anti-noble performance. The implicit acceptance of anti-noble performance by a team's leadership is an insidious disease that undermines and defeats a team or organization from within — and, ultimately, strips that organization of any sense of nobility.

To avoid exhibiting "acceptance" of anti-noble performance, a leader's position toward that performance should be this: *It's vitally important that _every_ member of the team deliver outstanding performance. When some team members are delivering outstanding performance and one or more are not, then it impacts the _entire_ team and prevents the team from achieving our goal of outstanding TEAM performance.*

As previously stated, this applies when a person has the *wherewithal* — that is, awareness, ability, and resources — to perform desired performance but has *chosen* not to do it. (For discussion on creating awareness, ability, and resources, see "How to Eliminate Lack of Awareness …", pgs. 37–40.)

In conclusion, Steps 1 through 5 can be taken, but if Steps 6 and 7 aren't scrupulously executed, the process will not take, the team or enterprise will not rise to a level of nobility in the eyes of your team members.

The upshot of creating a noble venture is it will infuse your enterprise with three "Ps" — Purpose, Pride, and Passion.

PURPOSE = deliberate action directed toward a higher goal — that is, directed toward accomplishment of the Point of Pride.

PRIDE = that sense of satisfaction derived from being a part of pursuing or realizing a higher goal.

PASSION = the commitment, enthusiasm, and sense of urgency that impels team members to do what has to be done to achieve a higher goal.

Marketing Tie-in

If the Point of Pride can be defined in a way that makes it usable in marketing, so much the better. To have a sales-building effect the statement must define a *main beneficial difference* between you and your competitors. As such, it must be a "provable fact." For further info on defining a point of difference, see *Differentiate or Die* by Jack Trout and Steve Rivkin and/or *Full-force Conceptioning* by John Correll.

To Sum Up ...

If you, the leadership, are willing to make the necessary personal commitment and sacrifice, you can turn your business or enterprise into a noble venture for yourself and your team. By doing this you give team members an opportunity to derive a deeper measure of personal satisfaction from delivering desired performance. Which, in turn, builds their motivation to deliver an above-average *amount* or an above-average *quality* of desired performance on an ongoing basis — or to achieve performance *excellence*.

Yes! — the "secret" to motivating team members to excellent job performance is: **Make doing desired performance to be MORE REWARDING than doing undesired performance.**

When doing desired performance is more rewarding than doing undesired performance, desired performance HAPPENS.

Motivator **#9** is a way to bring this about.

Motivator #9:
Make desired performance a
teamship experience.

MANY PERSONS derive a positive feeling from being an active contributing member of a worthy team. For brevity, we'll call this positive feeling *teamship experience.*

Note: "Teamship" is a new word we coined to convey the concept of this Motivator #9.

For humans to derive teamship experience, three conditions are typically required: (1) being a member of a worthy organization or team, (2) playing an active important role that contributes to the growth and success of that team, and (3) being appreciated for one's contribution by one's fellow team members. Many persons enjoy the teamship experience a lot, and will diligently strive to have it.

So, to motivate team members to pursue desired performance, consider installing the conditions that enables team members to derive

teamship experience from doing desired perfor-
mance.

To accomplish that, do these five steps.

STEP 1: Install a team concept within your organization — that is, implant within the mind of every team member the concept of *"we are a TEAM."* Ideally, this step should commence near the start of each person's involvement with the organization, or in the recruitment and orientation phase. But if it wasn't done at that time, it's not too late to do it now. Then, periodically reiterate the importance of the team concept in your communications with team members.

STEP 2: Make each team member realize that this team is a *special* team. Explain what makes the team unique from other teams. Describe the good things, or the accomplishments, that the team does that other teams aren't doing. In short, make team members realize that they're part of a *great* team. (Note: This is partially addressed in the nobility concept described in Motivator #8).

STEP 3: Make team members aware of the team's overarching purpose, or ultimate goal. This becomes the Common Goal that all team members are, or should be, aspiring for the team to achieve.

STEP 4: Explain the connection between each team member's role on the team and achievement of the team's Common Goal.

Below is a link to a YouTube video that starkly illustrates those first four steps. The video depicts a 60-second talk that coach Bo Schembechler gave to one of his teams many years ago. As you know — or perhaps don't know — Schembechler (now deceased) was a football coach at University of Michigan for many years, and over that time became one of the winningest coaches in the sport. At the start of the video there's 30 seconds of Schembechler sound bites. If you happen to be a U of M fan, then enjoy it. If you're not such a fan, then either (a) enjoy it for the heck of it or (b) stoically ignore it — consider it a tiny price to pay for seeing perhaps the greatest 60-second video that has ever been captured on the importance and role of *The Team*. Lastly, as I'm sure you realize, although Schembechler is speaking to a football team, the core concept of this talk is applicable to almost any team or organization (with a little adaptation, of course). Here's the link to the video. The video's title is "The TEAM."

youtube.com/watch?v=7KOwLaCf0y0

STEP 5: Provide the resources and training that enables each team member to make a worthwhile contribution toward realization of the Common Goal. (Note: See Motivator #2 for details on providing resources and training.)

STEP 6: Arrange for each team member's good performance, or their contribution to realization of the Common Goal, to be periodically recognized and appreciated by the *entire team*. (Note: See Motivator #1 for insight on how to deliver recognition, appreciation, and praise for maximal effect.)

Ways to Foster Team-building Activity

Any activity that builds teamship, or contributes to realization of the Common Goal, we call a *team-building activity*. Examples of team-building activity include things such as: harmonious team member communications, productive team member relations, positive attitude toward fellow team members, assistance to fellow team members, encouragement and support of fellow team members, and participation in team activities. So, at this point a question arises: What might you specifically do to motivate team members to perform team-building activity? Answer: You apply one or more of the previously described performance motivators. Here are eight examples.

1 – When it seems that the team could benefit from having a greater amount of team-building activity being performed by team members, then apply positive reinforcement. Which means, be on the lookout for instances of team-building activity. And, whenever you witness such an instance make it into a RAP-receiving experience for the person performing the activity. That is, deliver recognition, appreciation, and/or praise to the person (Motivator #1).

2 – When a team member is having difficulty performing their role in the team, or is having difficulty maintaining a "good attitude" due to confronting unnecessary hassle that's diminishing their job performance, do what you reasonably can to identify and eliminate any needless hassle, thereby making it easier for the person to maintain an attitude that's conducive to performing team-building activity (Motivator #2).

3 – When a team member is having difficulty performing their role in the team, or is having difficulty maintaining a "good attitude" due to performing a job they derive little innate enjoyment from, do what you reasonably can to move them to a role or job assignment that's innately more enjoyable for them to do (Motivator #3).

4 – When it seems that team members aren't seriously adopting the team concept or aren't focusing enough on performing team-building activity, consider creating a differential pay program and making the performance of team-building activity a part of the performance bonus criteria for their job (Motivator #4).

5 – When it seems that team members aren't considering the performance of team-building activity to be an important part of their job, take time to get *personally involved* with them. That is, personally explain the importance of team-building activity, then do on-the-job training to equip them with the wherewithal to do it, then frequently observe their on-the-job performance, and, finally, respond with positive reinforcement, or RAP, whenever you witness an instance of team-building activity (Motivator #5).

6 – When it seems that team members aren't working as a team, or aren't pursuing team-specific goals diligently enough, then create a team pursuit, or a "work game," of the type described in Motivator #6.

7 – When it seems team members don't view the performance of team-building activity to be of any long-term consequence, create an intra-position advancement system and make the performance of team-building activity to be part of the criteria for intra-position advancement (Motivator #7).

8 – When it seems that team members aren't seeing any inherent value to the enterprise, or to their job, or to performing team-building activity, consider turning your enterprise into a noble venture and then positioning the team, and team-building activity, as a vital component to maximizing the success of that noble venture (Motivator #8).

The way you make doing desired performance to be more rewarding for team members than doing undesired performance is:

You (a) EXPAND the reward they derive from doing desired performance and (b) SHRINK the reward they derive from doing <u>un</u>desired performance.

When you expand the reward from desired performance and shrink the reward from undesired performance, a greater amount of desired performance HAPPENS.

A way to do this is explained in upcoming Motivator **#10.**

Motivator #10:
Reduce the net reward connected to undesired performance.

FIRST LET'S REVIEW. The way you motivate team members to choose desired performance over undesired performance is you either (a) make desired performance *more* rewarding or (b) make undesired performance *less* rewarding. Motivators #1–9 deal with the first strategy. This motivator #10 deals with the second one — making undesired performance less rewarding. Apply this motivator when a person is pursuing undesired performance because doing that particular performance is a "rewarding experience" for them.

How to Make Undesired Performance Less Rewarding

There are two ways to reduce the net reward that a person gets from doing undesired performance. The first way is to *expand* the downside, or painful consequences, connected to doing the performance. The second way is to *diminish* the upside or enjoyment the person is deriving from doing the performance.

I recommend that, if at all feasible, you avoid getting involved in expanding the downside or painful consequences the person derives from doing the undesired performance. Instead, focus on reducing the upside or enjoyment the person is deriving from the performance.

As previously stated, the upside of a performance is any compensation, event, communication, condition, situation, or opportunity the performer derives from doing the performance *and also* finds to be enjoyable or beneficial. To shrink the upside associated with a particular undesired performance, structure the (job) situation so that doing the undesired performance results in the particular upside *no longer occurring,* or no longer being derived from doing the undesired performance.

When this is done it can sometimes result in a brief burst of repeated undesired performance by the particular person involved. This is due to their desire to re-experience the enjoyable upside previously associated with doing the undesired performance. But, if the upside reduction remains constant or, in other words, the upside does not return, the burst of undesired performance will likely soon taper off and result in an overall reduction in the frequency of the particular undesired performance.

This takes us to a pivotal question: Why, in certain cases, does undesired performance have such a strong upside in the first place? Certainly no competent manager would deliberately create the upside of undesired performance. One reason is, sometimes the upside of undesired performance is created by *non-deliberate reinforcement* — that is, by the performer receiving some sort of inadvertent pleasure or "reward" as a consequence of doing the performance. This can cause a person to pursue the undesired performance with greater frequency or persistence.

Oftentimes this non-deliberate reinforcement of undesired performance happens when a company compensation program makes no distinction between types of performance. Or, in other words, it happens when employees receive as much pay for doing undesired performance as for doing desired performance. Or, put yet another way, it happens when they receive the same amount of pay for doing an average amount of desired performance as for doing an above-average amount of desired performance.

Other times the reinforcement occurs when fellow employees shower attention on the performer of the undesired performance.

In conclusion, whenever a stubborn performance problem exists — that is, where a particular undesired performance is chronically present — the correction strategy is twofold:

1. Enact measures that increase the net reward of *desired* performance. (In this case, desired performance is any performance that's the opposite of the offending undesired performance.)

<u>AND</u>

2. Find out what the upside of the undesired performance is for the person performing the undesired performance, then reduce or eliminate that upside.

Core Concepts Summary

WE CONCLUDE with the following summation.

To make your enterprise more effective at achieving progress and realizing enterprise goals you must get your team members, or employees, to achieve a greater amount of desired performance and a lesser amount of undesired performance.

To get team members to achieve a greater amount of desired performance (and lesser amount of undesired performance) you must create within them the *motivation* to do that.

To create motivation in team members to achieve a certain desired performance you must make doing that desired performance to be *more rewarding* than doing undesired performance, in the eyes of the team members. Or, put more simply, you must *increase the net reward* team members derive from doing desired performance.

To increase the net reward team members derive from doing desired performance you must *increase the upside* and *decrease the downside* associated with doing desired performance.

To increase the upside and decrease the downside of doing desired performance you apply one or more of the following motivators. Or, more specifically, you manage in a way that makes desired performance to be:

1. A *RAP-receiving* experience (p. 25),

2. A *hassle-free* pursuit (p. 34),

3. A *fun* time (p. 42),

4. A *dollar-producing* endeavor (p. 48),

5. An *important* accomplishment (p. 60),

6. A *winning* situation (p. 64),

7. A personal *advancement* opportunity (p. 67),

8. A *noble* venture (p. 71), and/or

9. A *teamship* experience (p. 80).

   Plus ...

10. You *reduce* any upside that might be associated with doing <u>un</u>desired performance (p. 89).

In our view, these are the "Top 10 Motivators" for creating excellent team member performance and job satisfaction.

Now it's up to you. Pick one and try it out.

One last time — the "secret" to motivating team members to excellent job performance is:

Make doing desired performance to be MORE REWARDING than doing undesired performance.

When doing desired performance is more rewarding than doing undesired performance, desired performance HAPPENS.

Motivators **#1–10** are ten methods you can use for helping bring this about.